Why Me?

Surviving the
Hillsborough Disaster
1989

Robert C Lynch

i

DEDICATION

I dedicate this book to my amazing son Sam.
Every day is a blessing and I am forever thankful.

CONTENTS

ONE YEAR EARLIER 8

ONE YEAR LATER...12

JOURNEY TO HILLSBOROUGH.........................16

NO PREMONITION 21

SOMETHING STRANGE 27

MATCH ABANDONED 36

ARRIVING HOME 41

THE AFTERMATH 45

APPORTIONING BLAME..................................56

JUSTICE AND THE REAL TRUTH 65

v

ACKNOWLEDGEMENTS

My sincerest thanks must go to the Hillsborough Family Support Group and the Hillsborough Justice Campaign, who worked tirelessly to uncover the truth about what happened at Hillsborough in 1989. They persevered for over two decades to eventually clear the names of their loved ones. I must also express my appreciation of the Hillsborough Independent Panel, whose findings started an historic sequence of events that eventually unearthed a shameful cover-up and the overturning of the original inquest verdicts. This allowed survivors like me, to hold our heads up high and no longer carry the guilt of feeling that we had somehow contributed to the deaths of our fellow fans.

ONE YEAR EARLIER

I've never spoken about this before. Perhaps I should have and maybe in some strange way, I will feel better for having told my story.

We have to start off one year earlier, because a rather uncanny sequence of events took place at that time. It was 9th April 1988 and Liverpool had been drawn against Nottingham Forest in the semi-final of the FA Cup. It was a tough draw because both sides were strong, but this was only to be expected at such a late stage of the competition. The game was to be played at Hillsborough stadium, which was the home of Sheffield Wednesday football club.

The Football Association had concerns about potential hooligan activity and had decided that Liverpool fans should be given the smaller Leppings Lane end of the ground, whilst

Nottingham Forest fans would be given the larger Spion Kop end of the ground. The thinking behind this decision was that rival fans would not have to cross paths, as they made their way to their respective entry points. However, Liverpool football club was extremely unhappy with this decision, primarily because it meant that Liverpool would have some 6,000 less fans at the match, and as Liverpool's average home attendance was almost double that of Nottingham Forest, it seemed unfair that the club with the larger support should have less tickets.

Live broadcasts of football matches hardly ever took place in those days, so you either went to the games or you watched the 'Match of the Day' highlights on a Saturday night. During the eighties, I was a season-ticket holder at Liverpool FC, so I was fortunate enough to be able to attend all Liverpool home games, mostly with my dad.

Dad and I only ever went to a handful of away games and as this particular game involved travel, we decided not to bother on this occasion. Instead, I found myself sitting on a bar stool in the local betting shop on a Saturday afternoon, listening to the match radio commentary, whilst watching my fifty pence place-pot bet crumble! It was an enthralling match and Liverpool ended up winning the game 2-1. As the full time score appeared on the screen, everybody was punching the air in jubilation and total strangers were hugging each other! I was so excited because Liverpool had reached the the FA Cup Final and better still, it would be played at Wembley stadium! Reaching Wembley was no mean feat and the chance of winning the most prestigious of cups, was really something to look forward to.

That Saturday evening, I was in the 'Cock & Bottle' Public House on Wavertree High Street, when suddenly, a gang of lads came bouncing through the door. They were very noisy and I soon realised that some of them were my friends and they had just returned from Hillsborough. They had rushed back to celebrate Liverpool's fabulous win and we all had a great time. The atmosphere was electric and we sang football songs all evening. It would be fair to say that a decent amount of beer was consumed for the rest of that night. However, my joy was tinged with a slight feeling of regret and I felt as though I had missed out on something special. That night, I swore that I would never miss out on a big football occasion like this again. I went home and watched the recording of Match of the Day with my dad.

The next morning, I watched the recorded highlights of the game with my dad again and I asked him if he fancied going to the cup final at Wembley and we agreed that we would try, but we both knew that it would be difficult to get cup final tickets, because the ticket allocations were always so low. Unfortunately, we were unable to get tickets on that occasion because our season ticket serial numbers didn't qualify. However, I remember feeling a sense of relief on cup final day, because Liverpool lost!

ONE YEAR LATER

One year later, an extremely exciting Liverpool FC were performing well on all fronts and many believed that this team, consisting of players such as Barnes, Beardsley, Aldridge and Houghton, was one of the most exciting Liverpool teams ever produced. They were well on course to become English league champions once again and they were also on a good cup run. They had reached the FA Cup semi-final for the second year running and incredibly, they would play Nottingham Forest. The game would ironically take place at Hillsborough stadium in Sheffield, but this year had the potential to be extra-special, because Liverpool's local rivals Everton had reached the other semi-final. If both teams could win their respective semi-finals, they would face each other in an all-Merseyside FA Cup final at Wembley stadium!

Liverpool's history in the FA Cup had been relatively poor in real terms, as they had only won the competition three times in their illustrious history and they would generally have more success in the league and in Europe. However, since the 1985 Heysel disaster, all English clubs were banned from European competition for five years and with one less competition to contend with, Liverpool were able to focus more on the FA Cup.

I was extremely lucky, because it might have taken many years for Liverpool to reach another cup semi-final, but now was my chance to make up for the disappointment of missing out on the previous year.

I waited eagerly for the Liverpool Echo to publish the ticket information and a few days later, I was overjoyed to read that numbers five and six were the first qualifying numbers for a semi-final ticket. By pure chance, those numbers matched our season-ticket serial numbers and as ticket allocations were always larger for semi-final matches, we stood a great chance of getting tickets for the game. Dad was quite laid-back about most things and he remained poker-faced about the whole situation. I'm sure that deep down, he was as equally as excited as I was.

On the day that the tickets were due to go on sale, I took the day off work and I drove to Anfield, two hours before the ticket office opened. I was convinced that I would be the first person there and I couldn't believe it when I saw that a queue of a couple of hundred people had already formed! I couldn't relax until I reached the ticket office window, but the line moved quickly and before too long, I was the excited owner of two highly-sought after, FA Cup semi-final tickets. I raced home as quickly as I could, imagining that everybody was staring at me, because they knew I had those tickets.

For the next two weeks, I discussed the upcoming match with friends and work colleagues. Many of them were going to the game too and the tension was building as each day passed. Every evening, I would come home from work, take the tickets out of their hiding place and simply gaze at them.

As the match drew nearer, Dad and I discussed how we should travel to Hillsborough and we weighed up whether to get a coach, a train or to drive. Travelling by coach would be relatively cheap, but it always seemed to take an age to get to your destination and it wasn't the most comfortable of options. The train idea was quickly disregarded, when we discovered that there were connections involved. In the end, we decided that driving would allow us to travel at our leisure, though I was a little bit nervous, having never driven such a distance before. I had hoped that Dad would offer to drive, but he was having none of it and I was designated as the driver!

The evening before the game, I sat and stared at my ticket, whilst studying every detail on the front and back. I felt like Roald Dahl's Charlie Bucket, having just won the last remaining golden ticket. This ticket had only cost six pounds, but I wouldn't have sold it for six thousand! I was so lucky!

JOURNEY TO HILLSBOROUGH

The next morning, Dad and I got up at 8:00 a.m. and I was bouncing with child-like excitement. The weather appeared to be glorious and there wasn't a cloud in the sky. I was eager to start our journey as soon as possible and Dad was really annoying me, as he had to complete his ritual of consuming three cups of tea and two hard-boiled eggs, before we could leave. It took me less than two minutes to devour a bowl of Shreddies cereal, glazed with an inch of sugar.

I went outside to see what the weather was really like and I was delighted to find that it was lovely and warm, with glorious sunshine. This was not April weather as we knew it, but it simply was the perfect Spring day.

I asked Mum what she had prepared for

sandwiches and a look of horror came across her face. She had forgotten to buy our lunch the day before and within seconds; she dashed out of the house to get us something. I was quite annoyed by now, as I knew that this would delay us and I could not relax until we were on the road. Ten minutes later, she returned from the local shops with a bag of crusty cobs and.....crunchy peanut butter! She was so apologetic and explained that she hadn't been able to get any chicken or turkey for our sandwiches, so we had to settle for crunchy peanut butter. It would be fair to say that Dad and I were not impressed!

After checking the engine oil and water, We set off at 11:00 a.m. and I felt as though we had allowed plenty of time for any mishaps. I prayed that my old red mark three Ford Escort would at least get us to Sheffield. As far as I was concerned, it didn't matter if the engine exploded on the way home, just as long as we made it to the game!

The route was planned. We would take the M62 motorway to Manchester and then the A57 through Stockport and over the Pennines mountains to Sheffield. The motorway was bound to be the trickiest part, as our car had never been driven at high speed and it only had four gears. The engine was screaming like a banshee and I was anxious that it would not be able to take the stress for too long. The wheel tracking was well out and the steering wheel vibrated violently as we had exceeded fifty miles per hour.

It wasn't long before we hit heavy traffic on the M62, but that came as a slight relief, because I was able to drive at a much lower speed and rest the weary engine. The way I saw it was that as long as we kept moving, we were making progress and we were getting closer to Hillsborough. The main concern now was that the engine might overheat because it was so hot outside. I saw that many cars, newer than ours, had already broken down and were strewn along the hard shoulder. I felt so sorry for those individuals and wondered how on earth they were going to make it to the game.

Being a former mechanic, Dad came up with the

idea that we could release some of the engine heat, by turning the heaters on full blast - on the hot setting! The outside temperature was already in the seventies, yet we had to put up with hot air blowing in our faces - all the way to Sheffield!

Although the motorway traffic had moved quite slowly, when we joined the A57 at Stockport, it became a slow crawl. The only consolation was that we had the breath-taking mountain views to enjoy as we crossed the Pennines. We meandered up and down the hills in a single convoy of traffic and I observed red scarves hanging out of most of the car windows. It felt like we were part of an army, a huge pilgrimage, loyally following our team.

We eventually started to pick up signs for Sheffield, but the time had flown and it had already taken us almost three hours. There was a huge sense of relief as we spotted signs for Hillsborough and as we drove downhill into a valley, we spotted the stadium in the distance. At such a vantage point, it felt more like we were bringing a plane in to land, rather than driving a car.

It was already 2:10 p.m. and we had no time to relax, but thankfully, we found somewhere to park the car quite easily. There wasn't much time to eat, so we grabbed a quick bite of our crunchy peanut butter bread rolls and we began our walk downhill toward the stadium. It didn't take long for us to realise that we were walking alongside a large number of Nottingham Forest fans and I thought to myself, how ironic it was that the FA had wanted to keep supporters apart from each other and here we were, rubbing shoulders with the Nottingham Forest fans! We kept very quiet.

NO PREMONITION

We arrived at Leppings Lane at 2:20 p.m. and I noticed how the lane narrowed as we got closer to the stadium. Other than a little newsagent and a number of terraced houses, there was not a great deal else on Leppings Lane and it appeared to end at the stadium.

Outside the ground, we were presented with a brick wall which had a handful of turnstile entrances. But where were all of the fans? There were hardly any people around this entrance and only a couple of police officers. A female police officer asked us if we had tickets. I replied yes, but we weren't asked to show them. I reckoned that the majority of fans must already be inside the stadium, as it felt quite late now anyhow.

The stadium looked rather weary on closer

inspection. The brickwork looked shabby and the paintwork was flaky. We presented our tickets at one of the rickety turnstiles and found ourselves on the other side of the brick wall. As we faced the rear of the stand, we noticed that the only obvious entry point to the lower-standing tier was a tunnel through the middle of the stand. Above the entrance was a barely-legible sign that displayed the word 'STANDING', so naturally, we headed into the tunnel. It was pitch-black inside the passageway and I subconsciously ducked my head, as the ceiling was only marginally higher than my 6'4" height. Heading toward the daylight, I could see the bright green of the football pitch, a sight that made the hairs stand up on the back of my neck. As we reached the tunnel exit, we were suddenly faced with a wall of fans at the back of the terrace and we had to fight our way onto the standing area.

The first thing that I noticed was how packed the crowd was. We'd been in plenty of packed crowds before, so there was not really anything to be alarmed about at this stage. It was also an FA

Cup semi-final, so I suppose it was always going to be extra-busy for such a prestigious match. The second thing I noticed was that we were directly behind the goal, with its white net obstructing our view. It meant that we couldn't clearly see the central third of the football pitch.

It was a little uncomfortable by now and we were being jostled in every possible direction. But the atmosphere was electric and it was only half an hour until the scheduled kick off at 3:00 p.m. The crowd was singing loudly and occasionally, a balloon would float about our heads, before it was smacked in some random direction by an outstretched hand. It was extremely hot in the tightly-packed crowd and the occasional waft of fresh air was tinged with the sweet smell of tobacco smoke.

After a few minutes, Dad pointed out that the whole of the Leppings Lane terrace appeared to be split into four sections by three sets of iron railings. We were stood in one of the two middle sections, but what was very obvious was that the two outer pens were practically empty. After observing this, Dad suggested that we should move to one of the emptier outer pens, so that we could relax a little. I really didn't want to move and I would have preferred to stay where most of the singing was taking place, but after a heated discussion, Dad got his way. Had I gone to Hillsborough with somebody of my own age, there is no doubt that we would have remained in the central pen.

We fought our way back through the tunnel and exited to the main concourse. It took a moment to work out where to go, until we realised that it was possible to walk to the side of the stand and into a corner section.

There was a fire escape leading from the upper tier and dad and I agreed to meet there, in the likely event that we were separated during the game. We positioned ourselves next to the main stand, directly below the police box, and it immediately became obvious that we had made the right decision to move. The view was excellent and because we were higher up, we had a much better perspective of the playing field. I didn't say anything to Dad though, because I wanted to make him feel bad for forcing me to move!

Being so tall, I always liked to arrive at a half-empty terrace on good time, so that I wouldn't spoil anybody's view. Once I had my space, it was tough luck if anybody smaller got stuck behind me, because I was there first! I absolutely hated arriving late and spoiling somebody's view.

It was so empty that we were able to sit on the steps for a while and Dad was able to roll his cigarettes more easily. It was the typical pre-match ritual and I had to sit there, holding his tin and tobacco pouch, while he rolled enough cigarettes to last him for the duration of the game. Eventually, we stood up and looked around the stadium, taking in the atmosphere. The stands were filling up gradually and the noise level was increasing, with every passing minute.

Dad told me how he had visited Hillsborough on a few occasions during the sixties; mostly for cup matches and he specifically talked about an infamous FA Cup semi-final he'd attended. Liverpool had absolutely battered Leicester City, but their goal keeper Gordon Banks, had saved everything! I distinctly remember him saying that the stadium looked exactly how it had done, all those years ago and that other than a lick of blue and white paint here and there, nothing had changed.

Everything was perfect. Our view of the football pitch was unrestricted and it was a beautifully warm spring day. We were about to watch a classic semi-final match and a warm feeling of excitement came over me. I had no premonition of anything going wrong.

SOMETHING STRANGE

At 2:50 p.m. and after ten minutes of relative
comfort, there was a sudden rush of people onto
our terrace. They simply came from nowhere and
within seconds, our pen was completely full.
Luckily, we were standing by now and we
stumbled down several steps as the crowd surged
into us from behind. I assumed that this was the
rowdy lot that stays in the pub until the last
minute and comes pushing their way in to get the
best view. I was so angry that I pointed my
elbows and ran backwards up the steps, to push
back at those who had just pushed me. A man
said to me, "There's no need for that, there's
murder outside!" It didn't take me long to realise
that these people had not been drinking, as there
was no smell of alcohol and I realised that I had

been mistaken in my assumption. Perhaps there really had been a problem outside the stadium.

The players of both teams came onto the pitch and a massive roar came from the crowd. Suddenly, we were packed in like sardines and the crowd formed a vice-like grip around us, but it was bearable and we'd experienced worse. However, as I looked through the railings, which were about three feet to my left, I could see that things didn't look right in the centre pen – the one that we had left earlier! These people were not stumbling up and down nor were they swaying left or right. These people were packed together so tightly that there was no 'give' in the crowd. Normally, a typical crowd would open and close, as it swayed in different directions, but not this one. There was also a strange groaning noise coming from the crowd. It was so unlike the sound of a normal football crowd and occasionally, a high-pitched female shriek could be heard above the deafening hum. I could also see that there were two human feet per step, on steps which were only big enough to fit one set of feet. My attention was drawn from the crowd situation, back to the playing field, but I repeatedly found my gaze drawn back to what was happening to the left of me. Dad and I were about six feet apart by now and I was looking at the back of his head. I noticed that he was occasionally glancing left also.

The game kicked off and the focus of attention was back on the game. Within seconds, Liverpool were on the attack and Peter Beardsley hit a rocket of a shot from twenty five yards, that smashed against the Nottingham Forest crossbar. The massive roar from the Liverpool end caused the crowd to surge forward and we found ourselves even more tightly packed together. Little did we know that the thousands of people still outside the stadium were even more desperate to get inside, as they were now fully aware that the game had kicked off.

It still hadn't dawned on us that there was anything seriously wrong, when suddenly; a young lad appeared from nowhere. He had somehow managed to climb some nine or ten feet to the top of the overhanging perimeter fence. We soon noticed that other people were attempting to scale the pointed railings, as if to get onto the pitch. I thought to myself, 'Oh no, a pitch invasion, hooligans looking to spoil the game?' A police officer was stood at the fence with his baton drawn and he was hitting those climbing the fences, to stop them from making it over. The first lad appeared to fall back into the crowd and I never saw him again. Then came the realisation that something was wrong, because from the upper tier, people were hanging down and dragging fans up from the Leppings Lane terrace.

Liverpool goalkeeper Bruce Grobbelaar kept turning around and looking at the crowd. He had a concerned look on his face and seemed to be paying more attention to the fans behind the goal, rather than the game. There were now dozens of people on top of the iron fences and many were making it over and onto the edge of the pitch, behind the goal. A few of the patrolling police officers gingerly made their way toward the Liverpool end of the stadium and with a number of photographers in the same area, it started to get quite busy. The Nottingham Forest fans started booing and whistling loudly, obviously believing that this was some kind of trouble and an attempt to disrupt the game.

The mass of people behind the goal was growing quickly and some fans had no choice, but to encroach onto the actual playing area. Within minutes, the game was stopped by the referee and both teams were led off the pitch. It was clear that the players were annoyed at having to stop the game and some of them expressed their frustration toward fans who tried to approach them.

There were now many hundreds of people on the playing field and my first concern was that the game might not continue. Even now, we still had no concept of the enormity of the situation and I really hoped that the fans could be relocated back into the crowd. We had no idea that people had been injured - let alone killed.

More and more people were being brought onto the pitch. Some were limping, whilst others were being helped by fellow fans. One man walked onto the pitch, then immediately collapsed, spinning around as he fell. Some police officers had by now realised that there was a problem and they were attempting to help fans out, through a tiny opened gate. I observed that some fans were being physically carried and laid out onto the pitch and this could only mean that the level of injury was greater than I had first imagined. The penny finally dropped when I saw people being given mouth-to-mouth resuscitation.

I will never forget a little boy, who could only have been eight or nine years of age, laid on his back, with a man trying to resuscitate him. Everybody seemed to zoom in on this small child. He was wearing a Liverpool shirt and a pair of jeans. The soles of his little white trainers pointed toward me, whilst the man performed chest compressions and administered ventilation. Suddenly, a massive cheer and applause came from the fans in the adjacent Main stand as it appeared that the boy had been saved. A great sense of relief washed over me as the child was placed into the recovery position and I now felt sure that he would be okay; however, I still found myself worrying about how many other people had been injured. My attention was again drawn to my left and by now there were many hundreds of people on the pitch. A moment later, I looked right once more and, to my horror, I could see that the little boy was lying on his back again, but this time he had a coat over his tiny, still body. Surely the boy wasn't dead? How could this happen? How could a small child be dead? And if he could die, that meant other people could be dead! It made no sense - how could people DIE at a football match?

I wanted to get onto the pitch. I looked up at the spikes at the top of the fences and wondered if I could possibly climb such a foreboding obstacle. Could I be of any help? Would I get in the way? I felt frozen to the spot, totally unsure of what to do for the best.

The Liverpool end of the ground was awash with fans by now and it seemed that many, like me, were unsure of what to do. Some people were tending to the injured, others were attempting to pull down the fences to free those trapped, but many were just aimlessly wandering around in total shock. Some fans had climbed up the pitch-side of the fences, in an attempt to drag people out, but there was no sign of any medical help. A few police officers in close proximity were doing their best - they too were clearly in a state of shock as they had, by now, realised the gravity of the situation. However, there was also a large cordon of police officers traversing the entire pitch at the half-way line, as though they were expecting some sort of violence.

Fans started to take matters into their own hands. They formed teams of bearers, carrying the dead and injured, using advertising hoardings as make-shift stretchers, across to the far end of the pitch. I could hear the sound of emergency sirens from outside the stadium, but saw only one ambulance make it inside. It was a St John's ambulance and it looked like something from World War II. It ambled its way across the pitch and parked behind the goal, but it seemed like a hopeless exercise, because there were so many people laid out on the pitch and one ambulance clearly wasn't going to be enough.

Suddenly, our attention was drawn to the right again. We were standing very close to the police box and the crowd started to shout angrily toward the steps leading up to it. Walking lethargically up those steps was Graham Kelly, the Chief Executive of the Football Association. He had been amongst those responsible for assigning Liverpool fans to the Leppings Lane end of the stadium and he was bearing the brunt of their anger.

My thoughts of a football match had well and truly disappeared by now and I had started to realise that we were in the midst of a disaster.

MATCH ABANDONED

By 3:40 p.m. the crowd in our pen had thinned out considerably and Dad and I were stood together again. For the first time, we were able to talk about what we were witnessing and we tried to make some sense of the whole thing. It was highly likely that the game was not going to resume and Dad and I agreed that even if there was a game, we didn't want to be there any longer. There were bodies all over the pitch, some covered, others not. Clearly there had been fatalities and as we couldn't get onto the pitch to help, we decided the best thing to do was to leave the stadium. A sense of shame came over me for not being able to get to those people and help them in some way, and for feeling lucky that I had not fallen victim to the dreadful fate that others had suffered.

Surprisingly, there were hardly any fans outside the stadium, so we must have been amongst the first to leave. We hurriedly made our way back up Leppings Lane and headed in the direction of where we'd parked the car. We walked in total silence and I was numb from what I had just witnessed. The entire thing had seemed surreal somehow, like a bad dream. It was inconceivable that people had died right in front of our eyes!

After all of this, it never once occurred to either of us to phone home to tell Mum that we were safe. We wouldn't have had a clue where to find a telephone box and these were the days before mobile phones. In our defence, we didn't think mum would know what had happened anyway, because we had no idea that the whole thing had been broadcast on national television. As we arrived back at the car, a sense of panic set in and I felt an overwhelming urge to get us away from that Hillsborough as quickly as I could. Pulling away, we passed many fire engines hurtling past us in the opposite direction toward the stadium, but still we saw no ambulances. I switched the radio on immediately, to find out more about what was going on. I recall not really knowing in which direction we were headed, I just drove us uphill as fast as I could to get us out of that valley!

In no time at all, we were back in the beautiful Pennines mountains and the sun was setting directly in front of us. Dad was getting frustrated trying to tune the radio, because the local FM radio stations seemed to be playing nothing but music and the medium wave stations may as well have been broadcasting from the surface of Mars! Eventually, the first radio news bulletin came through, stating that seventeen people had been killed in the crowd crush. Dad shouted, "Seventeen!" We couldn't believe it. The bulletins were coming through every twenty minutes or so throughout our journey and the next one said twenty seven people had died. Then forty five! Then fifty three! I couldn't take in what I was hearing. Another disturbing part of these bulletins was that the news broadcaster had stated that Liverpool fans had broken down an exit gate to gain entry to the stadium, thus causing the crush. We had no reason to disbelieve what we were hearing at that time and I personally felt a sense of shame, that the actions of mindless individuals could have caused this disaster.

However, the story of the broken exit gate would change dramatically, later that evening.

As we came out of the mountains, I thought about the people we had seen on the way to Hillsborough, who had broken down and were stranded on the hard-shoulder of the M62 motorway. Were any of them killed? Did anybody not actually make it to the game? I pondered on the irony of how they may have cursed their bad luck, only to realise later, that it had been a blessing. I also remember looking at the traffic heading in the opposite direction to us and wondered if we were passing any relatives of those that hadn't been as lucky as we had been.

We passed through a few small towns and I observed a number of people going about their own business. I felt quite angry at this point. Didn't they know that a disaster had just taken place? Didn't anybody care? How dare they carry on as if nothing had happened!

In between the news updates, music was playing. But as it was quite mellow music, we just left it playing on a low volume. I will always remember one song that was played, called 'Holding back the Years', by 'Simply Red'. Somehow the lyrics to that song seemed so poignant. Not a word was spoken for the rest of that journey home.

ARRIVING HOME

We finally arrived home at 7:40 p.m. and we both walked into the back living room, to find Mum sitting with my uncle Jock. Jock was a jovial chap and he always had a smile on his face, but the solemn look on his face that day said it all. He would often call in on a Saturday afternoon, but he wouldn't normally stay longer than an hour. On this occasion however, he had decided to stay with mum until we returned.

As Dad and I walked into the living room, both Mum and uncle Jock stood up and I vividly recall Jock letting out a sigh of relief, whilst he patted me on the back of my shoulder. There were no hugs nor embraces, no smiles, or tears, just a huge sense of relief and overwhelming disbelief that something like this could have taken place at a football match.

I was quite surprised that the pair of them had been aware of what had happened, as they wouldn't normally follow the football, but they explained that the whole event had been broadcast on national television and radio. Mum mentioned that she had been out shopping earlier, when she noticed a number of shoppers gathered around a portable television. She asked one of the staff what had happened and a lady replied that there had been trouble at Hillsborough. That didn't alarm Mum, because she knew that we'd gone to Sheffield – she had never heard of Hillsborough! It wasn't until Jock arrived that he explained the situation to her. I asked Mum if she had been worried, but she replied that all she could think about was that she hadn't been able to get us our proper sandwiches to take with us!

The next few hours were spent moping around and not really knowing what to do with myself. I sat and wondered what on earth had gone wrong to cause such a tragedy at Hillsborough. I was still totally numb and despite knowing on an intellectual level that people had actually died, the magnitude of the disaster hadn't sunk in. The rest of the evening was spent following news updates.

Dad went to bed for an hour, but he came down to watch the nine o'clock news. The number of dead was now being reported as 72! We were astounded. We were also aware that there were an awful lot of people injured and that the death toll could rise further.

At 10:30 p.m. we sat glued to the television, for Match of the Day was about to start. They were meant to be showing the highlights of the two semi-final matches that evening, but it was quickly announced that no football matches would be shown on this sad occasion. The presenters wore dark suits and black ties and they began discussing what may have gone wrong at Hillsborough. The shocking news was now delivered that 94 people had been killed in the crowd crush. It began to hit us by now and I will never forget Dad saying "This is the worst day of my life!"

If anything positive could be taken from that

broadcast, it was the announcement that hooliganism had not played any part in this disaster and that the exit gate had not been broken down by Liverpool fans. In fact, the gate had been opened on the orders of the police.

Dad and I sat up into the early hours and although we didn't say a great deal, it just didn't feel right to go to bed. I think I was also fearful of sleeping, because I worried how I would feel the next morning. I sat on the couch staring at my match ticket stub, recalling how fortunate I had felt for having obtained it.

We never realised it at the time, but somewhere in our subconscious minds, Dad and I were 'done' with football that day. We never spoke about it as such, but I am sure that we both shared the same thoughts and feelings about our experience at Hillsborough. Dad and I never went to a football match again.

THE AFTERMATH

On the following Monday, I went to work as normal. It was very difficult to concentrate on work issues and my colleagues kept asking me if I was alright. No doubt it was the same for my work friends who had also been at Hillsborough.

By the following Wednesday, our shock turned to anger and dismay, when the Sun newspaper printed a front page headline of 'The Truth', stating that the whole terrible tragedy had been caused by drunken hooligan Liverpool fans and that they had been picking the pockets of the dead and dying. It was also claimed that Liverpool fans had urinated on the police officers and attacked them as they attempted to administer resuscitation. These unfounded allegations were viewed as a personal attack on the entire city of

Liverpool and, for more than two decades, the views of many thousands of people across the rest of the country would be tainted. The seeds of the 'myth of Hillsborough' had been sown and the people of Liverpool would not rest until the truth was known. Therein, lies the reason why most Liverpool newspaper outlets chose never to sell the Sun again and why so many people from Liverpool chose to never buy that newspaper again.

The next few weeks were spent watching news reports and any programmes mentioning Hillsborough. Every time the news came on, I watched the headlines eagerly, to see if there had been any developments. Nothing new transpired, but we knew that the overall process of investigation would be a slow one. I watched with pride as the bereaved families formed the 'Hillsborough Family Support Group', in an attempt to support each other and to 'get organised', so that their collective voice could be heard more loudly. HFSG still exists to this day!

A month after the disaster, Lord Justice Taylor

began the official inquiry into the Hillsborough disaster. We felt some kind of relief that at last, there would be a thorough investigation into the causes of the tragedy. His final report was published in January 1990 and it cast a scathing attack on the policing at Hillsborough. The crux of his report came in one sentence: *"Failure to close access to the central tunnel, before the exit gates were opened, was a blunder of the highest magnitude"*. He also stated that drunkenness had played no part in the disaster and that most of the fans were not affected by alcohol.

We were delighted with these findings and for the first time, believed that there might not be a cover-up after all. We looked forward to the repercussions of the Taylor report and thoroughly believed that the story of 'drunken hooligans' was finally dispelled.

Following the Taylor report, I by now had a better understanding of how the Hillsborough disaster had occurred. I spent a lot of time thinking about how lucky I had been to survive the disaster, whilst at the same time wondering, 'why me?' Why did I survive? Was it down to luck that I had escaped? What if Dad hadn't wanted to move? What if I'd gone to the game with my cousin instead? I felt a deep sense of guilt that I had been given the right to carry on living, whilst many men, women and children had not been granted such a precious gift.

In April 1990, the official inquests into the disaster commenced. To our dismay, these proceedings seemed to concentrate on alcohol levels and we were further perturbed when the coroner announced a 'cut-off' point of 3:15 p.m. This basically implied that all of the victims were either dead or fatally injured by that time. Something didn't feel right about the snippets of news that were coming from the inquest hearing.

A massive blow occurred in August 1990, when the Director of Public Prosecutions announced that there would be no further action regarding Hillsborough and that there would be no criminal proceedings, due to insufficient evidence! It didn't make sense. How could the DPP say that there was not enough evidence, when the Taylor report had clearly stated that lack of police crowd control had caused the tragedy? Surely the failure of the police to close the central tunnel was in itself, gross negligence! Furthermore, how and why would the DPP make this statement, before the inquests had finished? The decision not to take further action was a huge setback, because it felt like those individuals responsible had got away with it.

It wasn't about money and we weren't baying for blood. We just wanted somebody to be held to account for what went wrong. I swear that had the police hierarchy held up their hands in the first instance and said, 'we're so sorry, we screwed up and regret our mistakes', this whole saga wouldn't have dragged on for quarter of a century! Of course, some individuals would possibly have faced criminal proceedings, but wouldn't it have been better for those individuals to hold up their hands and clear their own consciences? Surely that would have saved them years of personal grief? My immediate thoughts were that there was going to be a cover-up and the earlier slur campaign would result in Liverpool fans being blamed for the disaster.

In March 1991, the inquest jury returned to deliver its verdict. We reacted with horror, as it was determined that the 96 Liverpool fans died as a result of accidental death. This couldn't be happening. Nobody set out to kill anybody that day, but people were responsible for the things that went wrong. This was certainly no accident. Can you imagine sending your own child to a pop concert and through a mistake of the organisers, they were killed? Would that be accidental death? Not a chance! There would have been culpability involved and somebody held to account. I knew in my heart that football fans were an easy target to pin the blame to. The underlying issues could easily be clouded by the fact that all football fans were drunken yobs and scum-of-the-earth lowlifes that brought this upon themselves! It felt like the door to justice had been well and truly slammed shut.

In the years that followed, every effort felt like it would be a waste of time. Some of the victims' families petitioned for new inquests, but those requests fell on deaf ears. Every application was rejected out of hand and the whole subject of Hillsborough began to feel very depressing. The general public was sick of it and even I was sick of it – sick because of how we had been left to feel that we had contributed to human deaths!

For years, Liverpool fans displayed banners at home and away matches, demanding justice for the 96 victims who went to a football match and never came home. They would have to endure years of torture, as opposition fans would chant about us being murderers and how we killed our own fans. It was hard to take. It seemed as though only the city of Liverpool knew the real truth and that the rest of the country had chosen to believe the lies that had been skilfully spun in those early days, following the disaster.

In December of 1996, a 'Jimmy McGovern' TV Drama was aired on national television, depicting the events of the Hillsborough disaster and how it affected the victims and the families of the victims on a personal level. Dad and I watched the programme with Mum and although it was particularly difficult to revisit Hillsborough, we were compelled to watch. The drama really brought home to us what it must have felt like to lose a loved one on that dreadful day. The drama won wide acclaim from the British public and even some television awards. It felt to me that the television dramatisation of the Hillsborough disaster had generated a lot of sympathy, but there were still many individuals who had already decided which version of events to believe.

In May 1997, Anfield stadium hosted a benefit concert named 'Rock the Kop', designed to raise money for the Hillsborough Family Support Group. Everybody involved provided their services for free and all profits went to HFSG. The turnout was impressive and the concert was broadcast on television a week later. It started to dawn on me that perhaps this concert, just like the television drama, was preventing the memory of Hillsborough from being buried. It was all publicity and every time something like this was aired nationally, it served as a good reminder to certain individuals that this was not going to go away.

A month after the concert, the Home Secretary – Jack Straw - announced to parliament that there would be a scrutiny of all evidence relating to the Hillsborough disaster. It felt like a positive step, as we were now served by a Labour government and many believed this to be the political party of the people. Jack Straw appointed Lord Justice Stuart-Smith to oversee the scrutiny during October of 1997. However, alarm bells began to ring, the moment he arrived in Liverpool. As he met a handful of the relatives of the victims, he asked where the rest of the families were and he questioned if they were going to turn up late, like the Liverpool fans! In actual fact, the rest of the families were upstairs, as there was some confusion about the meeting point. It wasn't a good start to proceedings and people started to suspect that they were perhaps being led down a familiar path. The following February, the families were told that no new evidence had been revealed and that the enquiry would go no further. The matter was now deemed as 'closed'. Once again, there was a huge feeling of dejection and everybody connected to Hillsborough felt that the Labour party had let them down.

A splinter group named The Hillsborough Justice Campaign emerged in 1998, representing some of the bereaved families that were not part of the Hillsborough Family Support Group. This also allowed survivors of the disaster to have a voice. Things were quite organised now and with various funding in place, the families of the Hillsborough victims decided to pursue a private prosecution against David Duckenfield and Superintendent Bernard Murray. They would be tried for manslaughter at Leeds Crown Court. To our surprise, it was quickly decided that neither defendant would face the possibility of imprisonment if found guilty, due to them being police officers. Proceedings were extremely slow and we followed developments over the next couple of years, catching any news bulletins that cared to report on it. In July 2000, Bernard Murray was found 'not guilty' of manslaughter and no verdict was reached with regard to David

Duckenfield. We were left with a feeling that this had been a 'show trial' and that the truth was never going to emerge.

Liverpool fans did not give up. The Hillsborough banners and flags were displayed at all games and chants such as, 'Justice for the 96' never ceased. However, it seemed that the public were growing weary about the mere mention of the word 'Hillsborough' and every now and then, a high profile figure would pop up and declare that they were sick to death of the subject of Hillsborough.

APPORTIONING BLAME

On the 15th April 1989 at Hillsborough stadium, 94 people had died, plus two seriously injured fans died after the event. The total number of fatalities was 96.

Who was to blame? This is still an argument today and whilst I can only offer my own opinion about this, I feel that as a witness, I am qualified to do so.

Like all disasters, there was no single cause of this tragedy. For a disaster to take place there would normally be a sequence of events or ingredients and they must occur in the correct order. The police were the highest authority and they must be held to account for the part that they played in this disaster. They had a duty of care, to create a safe environment for the spectators and on that day, it is my opinion that they failed in that duty of care.

At the 1988 semi-final, a police cordon was established at the top of Leppings Lane. That end of the lane was wide open and there was no real likelihood that a dangerous crowd could build up. Nobody was allowed to cross the cordon, until they had shown that they had a valid ticket. This cordon served two purposes: - Firstly, it ensured that anybody without a ticket could not get near to the stadium. Secondly, it allowed fans to trickle down to the turnstiles more slowly and as there were only a limited number of turnstiles to provide entry for 24,000 fans; a dangerous crowd did not build up outside the ground. No such cordon was set up at the 1989 match.

The police were ultimately responsible for the opening of the main exit gates, which allowed thousands of fans to enter onto the Leppings Lane terraces, even without showing their tickets. The police had determined that the crush developing outside of the stadium, represented a danger to life and thus, the order was given to open the gates on several occasions. This allowed thousands of fans at a time, to flood onto the main concourse of Leppings Lane. However, the decision to open the exit gates alone did not need to result in disaster.

From the main concourse, the only obvious entry point to the terraces was the central tunnel. Thousands of fans headed for that tunnel, which led to the two central pens. These pens were already overcrowded and there was simply no room for the torrent of fans approaching. Some fans spilled onto the already packed terraces, whilst many remained trapped in the tunnel. Had the police sealed off the tunnel entrance by closing the concertina doors, prior to opening the exit gates, the incoming fans could have been directed to the more sparsely populated side pens.

The regular match commander for Hillsborough had been suspended, only a few weeks prior to the 1989 game. This was as a result of a prank that went wrong, involving two of his officers. Chief superintendent David Duckenfield was given the role of match commander on that fateful day, but his level of experience as a match commander was minimal and could possibly explain the lack of police cordon and the tunnel not being closed.

The police were clearly not prepared for what was to unfold and it seemed as though they did not know what to do when it happened. This maybe because of a lack of planning or even training and it seems that the overall policing of the game was more geared to being ready for hooligan activity and not about ensuring spectator safety. Once again, the lack of an experienced match commander could have played a part in this confusion.

There was a definite breakdown in communication that day and the general feeling was that nobody knew how to deal with it. Without question, a number of police officers acted heroically and tried desperately to save people, whilst at the same time, a cordon of police was established at the half-way line, to deter potential hooligans from heading toward the opposing fans.

The Football Association should be held to account for the part that they played. For the second year running, Liverpool's fans were allocated to the Leppings Lane end of the stadium, which was the smaller end of the ground. This also meant that Nottingham Forest would have 6,000 more fans at the game than Liverpool. The tickets should have been allocated based on average 'home' attendance figures and at that time, Nottingham Forest's average home attendance was around 24,000, whereas Liverpool's average home attendance was around 40,000. Therefore, the demand for tickets at Liverpool was bound to be far greater than at Nottingham Forest. The reason why the FA would not budge on the ticket allocations was because they had concerns about the two sets of fans passing/meeting each other, despite the fact that we walked to the stadium with a large group of Nottingham Forest fans! - the hooligan approach again. However, there is a counter-argument here: A total of 24,000 fans needed to gain access to the Leppings Lane standing and seated areas, via Leppings Lane. It has now been scientifically proven that the number of fans without tickets situated at that end of the ground was negligible and did not have any bearing on the actual crush. The simple fact was that, since 24,000 supporters were bound to gain access via Leppings Lane, this number would have been the same, regardless of whether they were Liverpool fans, Nottingham Forest fans or anybody else's fans! It goes without saying that the Hillsborough Disaster could have happened during any match played there – as it almost did in 1981, when Tottenham fans suffered crushing injuries in a similar event.

Once it became apparent that the sheer numbers of people outside the stadium would not gain entry to the ground on time, the kick off time could have been delayed and an announcement made to those supporters. This may have helped to calm the situation outside the turnstiles at Leppings Lane. However, no such decision was taken by the police, nor the FA.

Many fans did arrive late on the day of the disaster. However, I can vouch that there were many delays along the route to Sheffield, mostly in the form of roadworks. I have often wondered why there had been no plans put in place to temporarily remove the cones, as there was clearly no work taking place.

The stadia of English football were well behind the times. Supporters were forced to put up with being penned into old-fashioned standing terraces and many fans from that era believed that they were being herded like cattle. It was obvious that revenue earned by the clubs was hardly being used to modernise stadiums.

Sheffield Wednesday football club contributed to this disaster indirectly. The stadium was old and decrepit and the lack of financial investment into the facility was there for all to see. However, they were no more guilty than the majority of football clubs in England at that time, because stadia as a whole was not entirely fit for purpose.

Perhaps the most damning fact revealed, was that the safety certificate for Hillsborough had expired some years before this game and therefore, no matches should have been allowed to take place at this stadium, until there was a valid safety certificate in place. Questions also have to be asked as to why the City Council allowed the stadium to continue operations without a valid safety certificate and the same question should be put to the Football Association. In retrospect, the game should have taken place at Old Trafford (Manchester United) – where ironically, the replay of this match was actually played.

The hooligan element within football had seriously damaged the reputation of ALL football fans and during the eighties, hooliganism was rife. As a consequence, we had perimeter fences penning us in. These were designed to segregate opposing fans and stop people from encroaching onto the pitch. I can honestly say that the fences at Hillsborough certainly did the job that they were designed to do.

Finally, we have the dynamics of a crowd. This disaster had nothing to do with a football match. It was more to do with crowd dynamics. If a crowd of thousands of people is heading for one place, there are bound to be dangers. Witnesses described how they were literally lifted off their feet and carried down the tunnel into the central pens. They had no control over this dynamic and the people at the front of those pens didn't stand a chance. This could just as easily have been a rock concert, a nightclub or a religious gathering.

Ultimately, the police were employed that day to oversee control of that crowd and to ensure safety.

JUSTICE AND THE REAL TRUTH

Every year, a memorial service would be held at Liverpool's Anfield stadium on 15th April. An average of 10,000 people would typically attend these events. However, the twentieth anniversary of the disaster saw a huge shift in proceedings. On 15th April 2009, over 25,000 people unexpectedly turned up at Anfield, taking everybody by surprise. The club was forced to open the remaining stands and the stadium was populated on all four sides. The strength of feeling had not faded away and in fact, had grown in monumental fashion. MP Andy Burnham was heckled by the crowd, as he attempted to deliver a speech on behalf of the government. The Culture Secretary was so affected by the events of that day, that he played a huge part in persuading the government to disclose all official documentation relating to the Hillsborough disaster - ten years earlier than normal. This documentation would be scrutinized by the Hillsborough Independent Panel.

The Hillsborough Independent Panel was set up by the government in January 2010, to examine the official documentation related to the Hillsborough disaster. Their job was to ensure that all of the facts regarding the disaster were released to the families of the deceased and then to the general public. Their work took over two years and when the panel completed their task, they published their findings in a report on 12th September 2012. Their findings highlighted the following:

1) Doubts were cast over the original inquest ruling of accidental death, as 41 of the 96 victims had the potential to survive – had they received adequate medical treatment.

2) South Yorkshire police and other emergency services, attempted to deflect the blame for the disaster onto Liverpool fans.

3) 116 out of 164 police statements were

amended, to remove comments that could be deemed as unfavourable to South Yorkshire police.

4)   Police carried out blood/alcohol examinations of the victims (including children), to further damage the reputation of the fans.

5)   Allegations that drunken Liverpool fans had contributed to the disaster were unfounded.

For your information, the report of the Hillsborough Independent Panel is in the public domain and the findings can be accessed easily online.

On the day that the Hillsborough Independent published its findings, it sent shock-waves around the world. I received dozens of text messages from close friends and family members, congratulating me for finally being vindicated of the dreadful lies that had been perpetuated by the media. The minds of many people had been polluted by a perceived truth and at last, the myth of Hillsborough was erased. My personal emotional release was overwhelming. I had to leave work early that day, for every few minutes, I would be reduced to floods of tears. Whilst trying to make sense of my emotional state, I realised that a huge black cloud had been lifted from my shoulders. The only way I can explain this is to use the analogy of somebody being released from a twenty-three year prison sentence, after being found innocent of a crime they didn't commit. At last, I was able to turn my back on the feelings of guilt that I had unwittingly carried with me for all those years – feelings that made me believe that I had somehow contributed to the deaths of the victims of Hillsborough.

Following the publication of the findings of the Hillsborough Independent Panel, Prime Minister David Cameron addressed the House of Commons and offered a heartfelt apology to the families of the victims of Hillsborough, for the injustice that they had endured for over two decades. The former editor of The Sun – Kelvin MacKenzie also offered an apology for the front-page publication of 'The Truth' story, published only four days after the disaster.

On 16th October 2012, Dominic Grieve –

Attorney General, announced that he would be applying to the High Court, to request a ruling that the original inquest verdicts of 'accidental death' be quashed and that new inquests be held into the 96 deaths at Hillsborough. On 19th December 2012, those original verdicts were quashed by the Lord Chief Justice – Lord Judge and new inquests were ordered.

On 31st March 2014, the new inquests into the 96 deaths at Hillsborough began - a process that would take a little over two years. The inquests took place in Warrington, so that the families had easier travel access to and from the venue, which they attended on a daily basis. On 26th April 2016, the inquest jury delivered its verdict and announced that all of the Hillsborough victims were 'unlawfully killed'. It was also decided that the match commander - Chief Superintendent David Duckenfield, was responsible for 'manslaughter by gross negligence', due to a breach of his duty of care. A criminal investigation into the disaster is ongoing.

I would like to thank you for reading my story

and I sincerely hope that it has been enlightening for you. Revisiting the Hillsborough disaster has been a very painful experience for me and many wounds have been reopened, recollecting my memories of that day. Perhaps witnessing the unfolding of a disaster of such magnitude never goes away from you.

I would like to end on a quote from Liverpool's former manager, Bill Shankly:

"Some people say that football is a matter of Life & Death. I say it is more important than that".

Saturday 15th April 1989 was the day that football became a matter of Life & Death.

RIP the 96 who lost their lives and justice for the families of those innocent victims.

ABOUT THE AUTHOR

Robert C Lynch began his career as a humble civil-servant, processing mortgage applications for tax relief.

After deciding to enhance his educational qualifications, he studied web design and multimedia, enabling him to become a self-employed web designer.

Inspired by his college lecturer, Robert enrolled on a teacher-training course at Liverpool John Moores University, attaining a Certificate of Education qualification. He went on to teach Computer Technology, Multimedia, English Language and Mathematics at a Liverpool College for many years.

Robert is currently a director of Bitwise Media LTD, coordinating IT training for clients.

Robert resides in the city of Liverpool, with his son

Sam.

If you would like to contact Robert to ask any questions regarding the Hillsborough disaster, you can email him at: robertclynch@gmail.com

Please note that a percentage of the sales of this book will be donated to the Hillsborough Family Support Group.

Printed in Great Britain
by Amazon

43256533R00043